cozy toes
for baby

Sweet Shoes to Crochet and Felt

Chantal Garceau and Mary J. King

Martingale

Create with Confidence

Dedication

To the Masheheni children and the Imani Project that introduced us, and to the happy synchronicity of creativity and philanthropy.

Linet, shown above, was the first Kenyan child I sponsored through the Imani Project, and the inspiration for my charitable enterprise, Chantal's Little Shoes. She is a teenage girl who loves learning and can attend school now that she has a uniform and her family has enough to eat. James is a nine-year-old orphaned boy who, along with his three siblings, can live with a guardian in his village instead of the distant orphanage, with financial support for the whole family. Shamsa, three, was not expected to live through infanthood with HIV and severe malnutrition, but received the medicine she needs and is now thriving in her grandmother's care. Baraka is a 16-year-old boy who proudly painted a sign for the village's first community toilet. The children of the village of Masheheni, in Malendi, Kenya, have inspired me to design these shoes and to write this book. Creating beautiful, useful gifts has always brought me joy, but it was compounded tenfold when I discovered that my shoes, and now this book, could bring so much to these very important people on the other side of the globe. The world became smaller and my heart became bigger.

~Chantal

Cozy Toes for Baby:
Sweet Shoes to Crochet and Felt
© 2014 by Chantal Garceau and Mary J. King

Create with Confidence

Martingale®
19021 120th Ave. NE, Ste. 102
Bothell, WA 98011-9511 USA
ShopMartingale.com

Printed in China
19 18 17 16 15 14   8 7 6 5 4 3 2 1

Library of Congress Cataloging-in-Publication Data is available upon request.

ISBN: 978-1-60468-458-2

Mission Statement

Dedicated to providing quality products and service to inspire creativity.

Credits

PUBLISHER AND CHIEF VISIONARY OFFICER: Jennifer Erbe Keltner

EDITOR IN CHIEF: Mary V. Green

DESIGN DIRECTOR: Paula Schlosser

MANAGING EDITOR: Karen Costello Soltys

ACQUISITIONS EDITOR: Karen M. Burns

TECHNICAL EDITOR: Ursula Reikes

COPY EDITOR: Marcy Heffernan

PRODUCTION MANAGER: Regina Girard

COVER AND INTERIOR DESIGNER: Connor Chin

PHOTOGRAPHER: Brent Kane

ILLUSTRATORS: Sue Mattero and Laurel Strand

Contents

Bonus Project Online! Download the pattern for Teddy Bear shoes at ShopMartingale.com/extras

A Journey Begins with a Little Shoe

From early girlhood on, I have been sewing, crocheting, and crafting, designing everything from sportswear to wedding cakes to garden architecture. My first felted baby shoes were gifts for delighted friends and family, and soon I was asked to make little shoes for charity auctions. As I pondered new directions in my work life and a meaningful use for my design talents, serendipity intervened. A casual chat led me to the Imani Project (www.imaniproject.org), and the connection felt right. I decided to sponsor a Kenyan child orphaned by HIV/AIDS.

My shoes' popularity encouraged me to sell them to help these children, which gave birth to Chantal's Little Shoes, a volunteer-driven company with the motto "Give a little love . . . give a little shoe." Coauthor Mary King, also looking for a way to merge her interests with service, joined me as a volunteer. The baby shoes are sold online and in Seattle-area markets, and now my products include Christmas ornaments and custom designs for corporations. Chantal's Little Shoes sponsors 10 orphans, allowing them to stay in their villages with foster families and receive the food, clothing, medicine, and school supplies they need. Additional proceeds, including those from your purchase of this book, go to support health, sanitation, and education projects in the children's communities.

In this book you'll learn to make seven of my designs, the cutest and coziest coverings imaginable for little feet, in sizes to fit newborns to age two. With thick felted forms, leather soles, and appealing character, these are a step beyond the time-honored baby bootie, worthy of becoming your family's new tradition for baby gifts. We've even included a gift card with care instructions on page 39 that you can photocopy to accompany your present of little shoes.

One basic pattern is used for all of the shoes, and they are all easy to make. Each shoe style is detailed with recommended colors and changes as well as finishing instructions for before and after felting. The basics of crochet and felting are explained with illustrations, along with savvy tips for success, so beginners can produce expert results. More advanced fiber artists will enjoy using the patterns as a springboard for further embellishment, or they may experiment with different sizes and fibers. You will find that each pair of shoes acquires its own personality and unique charm.

Crafters and artists can make an impact in the world. We hope the story behind these little shoes inspires you to use your own talents to make a difference too. You've already helped a child in Kenya by buying this book. Meanwhile, enjoy making and giving these cozy shoes for the littlest loves in your life.

~ Chantal

What You Will Need

Some of the materials and tools here are essential, while some can be improvised or substituted as described. Online resources for the supplies are listed on page 48.

Materials

Yarn. Medium worsted-weight 100% wool yarn is necessary to make the felted shoes. A great choice is Patons Classic Wool. The colors are lovely, it felts nicely, and it is very affordable. Cascade Yarns' Cascade 220 is another fine choice. These yarns are widely available. Don't use wool yarn labeled "superwash," as it won't felt.

Because one 220-yard skein of worsted-weight yarn is enough for at least two pairs of shoes, you may already have enough yarn left over from other projects to make one of the styles in this book. Just make sure that you choose medium worsted-weight 100% wool, or your gauge may be off and the shoes might not felt properly. Crochet a gauge swatch (see page 7) to see if the yarn will felt and how much shrinkage will occur.

Yarn used *after* the felting process, as finishing embroidery on the shoes, can be of any fiber type or weight. This is a great opportunity to raid your stash of yarn, including needlepoint yarn, or embroidery floss. If you have something that's the right color but a lighter weight, you may need to double or triple the strands to achieve the desired features. No stash? You can purchase "craft trim" at fabric and craft stores to use for finishing embroidery. It's yarn sold in 20-yard lengths, eliminating the need to buy an entire skein of the right color for details. Make sure the trims are washable so there will be no problem when the shoes are washed at a future date.

Leather. The shoes all feature leather soles, and the leather can be any color. Leather can be purchased at leather craft stores, on the Internet, and in some fabric stores. This is a perfect opportunity, however, to recycle a leather garment or handbag. Your local thrift store might yield a leather skirt or vest that can be obtained cheaply because of stains, yet has plenty of usable area to cut up for little shoe soles. Don't overlook the children's department! That little cowboy vest can be repurposed. The little shoes with leather soles can be machine washed.

Suede elbow patches are an easy option, and although they have a higher per-yard price than a split hide of suede leather, they may be just the ticket if you plan to make only one pair of shoes. They are sold in packs of two at fabric stores, and each patch is about the right size for one shoe.

Satin ribbon. This is used only for the Fresh Watermelon shoes (page 11 and below).

Tools and Supplies

You'll need a few different tools for the various assembly steps: crocheting, felting, making soles, and adding facial features.

FOR CROCHET

Crochet hook. Start with a size H-8 (5 mm) crochet hook and make a swatch to check your gauge (see "How to Crochet a Gauge Swatch," on page 7). Depending on your gauge, you may need a larger or smaller hook.

No Sore Fingers!

Comfort cushions for crochet hooks can make your crocheting more comfortable and enjoyable by reducing hand stress. A few companies manufacture versions of these inexpensive spongy cushions that fit over any size hook—our favorite is the Susan Bates Comfort Cushion—and they are available at most craft stores.

Needles. A darning needle will be necessary for weaving in tails of yarn after crocheting. Darning needles usually have a dull rounded tip, which is perfect for weaving in ends. You'll need a sharp yarn needle for embroidering details and for stitching the soles onto the shoes.

Pins. Ball-head straight pins are needed to hold soles and ears in place while stitching.

FOR FELTING

See "Felting" on page 34 for a list of the supplies you'll need.

FOR MAKING SOLES

See "Soles" on page 37 for a list of the supplies you'll need.

FOR ADDING FACIAL FEATURES

Plastic template material for making face stencils. You'll need a small piece of clear, slightly flexible plastic, which will make it easy to produce two shoes that look the same. You can recycle clear plastic packaging or a clear plastic sheet protector.

Small scissors or craft knife for cutting out the stencils for the face.

Pen or pencil for drawing the stencil on plastic.

Chalk pen or air-soluble pen for transferring facial features onto the shoe using the stencil.

The Basic Shoe Pattern

All of the little shoe styles are created from one primary pattern, described and illustrated in this section. You'll need to refer to this, along with the pattern specifics provided for the individual shoe styles; color changes and finishing touches provide the features unique to each. The shoes are crocheted all in one piece with no seams. Once you know how to make one style, you've got the skills under your belt to make any other pair of shoes in this book.

How to Crochet a Gauge Swatch

Obtaining the right gauge is very important to making little shoes that fit properly. It cannot be overemphasized! Make a gauge swatch so that you can adjust your stitch tension or your crochet hook to match the gauge stated in the pattern. You may need to repeat the process a few times until you obtain the correct gauge. Use the type of yarn and crochet hook specified in the pattern.

To easily remember where to make the first double crochet on a chain, crochet the first 14 chain stitches, pinch the chain at that point, then crochet three chain stitches. The last three chain stitches provide the height for the first double crochet. There will be 17 chain stitches total.

To begin, ch 14, pinch here, ch 3. (17 chs)

Row 1: Dc in 4th ch from hook (at the pinch), 13 dc to end. (14 sts)

Row 2: Ch 3, turn, 1 dc in 2nd stitch (fig. A). Skipping over the first stitch will produce a straight edge. Continue with one double crochet in the next 13 stitches, with the last double

crochet going into the top of the chain three (fig. B) from the previous row; again, this will produce a smooth edge.

Figure A

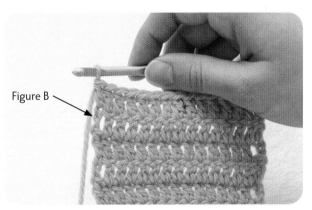

Figure B

Rows 3–8: Repeat row 2.

After 8 rows, your swatch should measure 4" x 4". If your gauge swatch *doesn't* measure 4" x 4", change crochet hooks. If your swatch is too small, use a larger crochet hook. If your swatch is too large, use a smaller hook.

The Basic Shoe Pattern

You'll see that your shoe lengths change after felting (they will shrink) and adding leather soles (they will stretch a bit).

SIZES

XS (S, M, L, XL)
To fit: 0–3 (3–6, 6–12, 12–18, 18–24) months
Length before felting: 5½ (6, 6½, 7½, 8½)"
Length after felting: 3¾ (4¼, 4½, 4¾, 5¼)"
Finished length with leather sole: 4 (4½, 4¾, 5¼, 5¾)"

GAUGE

14 dc and 8 rows = 4"

MATERIALS

1 skein (all sizes) of medium worsted-weight 100% wool yarn

H-8 (5 mm) crochet hook or size required to obtain gauge

MAKING THE SHOES

Make 2.

Rows 1 and 2 will form the base or sole of the little shoes.

Foundation ch: Make a slip knot, ch 14 (17, 20, 23, 26), pinch, ch 3—17 (20, 23, 26, 29) chs.

Row 1: Dc in 4th ch from hook (at the pinch), 1 dc in next 12 (15, 18, 21, 24) ch—13 (16, 19, 22, 25) dc with 1 ch rem. One side of sole is complete. Dc 7 in last ch, forming beg of toe box, working down other side of ch, 13 (16, 19, 22, 25) dc to create other side of sole—33 (39, 45, 51, 57) sts. Join with sl st to top of ch 3 to shape heel of sole.

Row 2: Ch 3, turn, 1 dc in same st as ch 3, 13 (16, 19, 22, 25) dc, 2 dc in *each* of next 7 sts to cont forming toe box, 12 (15, 18, 21, 24) dc, 2 dc in last st to cont forming heel—42 (48, 54, 60, 66) sts. Join with sl st to top of ch 3.

The sole of the little shoe is completed. This is the transition point from the sole to the sides and upper shoe.

Beginning of Rows

For most of the rows in the patterns, you'll begin the row with a number of chain stitches, and then start crocheting in the second stitch, not the stitch where the chain is coming from. In some patterns, however, you may be instructed to start the first crochet stitch in the same stitch where the chain stitches are coming from. Unless otherwise instructed, always start crocheting in the second stitch after the chain stitches. The chains beginning each row are to create height for the first stitch and do not count as a stitch, unless otherwise indicated.

Row 3: Ch 3, turn, beg in 2nd st, dc in *each* st—42 (48, 54, 60, 66) sts. Join with sl st to top of ch 3.

Row 4: Ch 3, turn, 16 (19, 22, 25, 27) dc, dc2tog 5 (5, 5, 5, 6) times, 16 (19, 22, 25, 27) dc—37 (43, 49, 55, 60) sts. Join with sl st to top of ch 3.

Row 5: Ch 3, turn, 12 (15, 18, 21, 23) dc, dc2tog 7 times, 10 (13, 16, 19, 23) dc, 2 (2, 2, 2, 0) dc in last 1 (1, 1, 1, 0) st—31 (37, 43, 49, 53) sts. Join with sl st to top of ch 3.

Row 6: Ch 3, turn, 9 (12, 14, 18, 20) dc, dc2tog 6 (6, 7, 6, 6) times, 8 (11, 13, 17, 19) dc, dc2tog—24 (30, 35, 42, 46) sts. Join with sl st to top of ch 3.

Sizes XS and S only

Row 7: Ch 2, turn, 8 (9) sc, sc2tog 4 (6) times, 8 (9) sc—20 (24) sts. Join with sl st to top of ch 2.

Row 8: Ch 2, turn, 20 (24) sc, join with sl st to top of ch 2.

Row 9: Ch 2, turn, 20 (24) sc, join with sl st to top of ch 2. Fasten off.

Size M only

Row 7: Ch 2, turn, 10 sc, dc2tog 7 times, 8 sc, sc2tog. (26 sts) Join with sl st to top of ch 2.

Row 8: Ch 2, turn, 26 sc, join with sl st to top of ch 2.

Row 9: Ch 2, turn, 26 sc, join with sl st to top of ch 2. Fasten off.

Sizes L and XL only

Row 7: Ch 2, turn, 15 (16) sc, dc2tog 6 (7) times, 13 (14) sc, sc2tog—35 (38) sts. Join with sl st to top of ch 2.

Row 8: Ch 2, turn, 11 (12) sc, dc2tog 6 (7) times, 10 sc, sc2tog—28 (30) sts. Join with sl st to top of ch 2.

Row 9: Ch 2, turn, 28 (30) sc, join with sl st to top of ch 2.

Row 10: Ch 2, turn, 28 (30) sc, join with sl st to top of ch 2. Fasten off.

Which Side Is the Right Side?

Before weaving in yarn ends, you'll need to choose a right side (RS) and wrong side (WS). After crocheting both shoes, turn one shoe to one side and one shoe to the other. Compare the lines of color change. Which one looks neater with a clearly defined pattern? Whichever side you choose as "right," make sure that both shoes match. Use a safety pin to mark the right side. Compare the top fronts of the shoes below.

Shoe on left is wrong side. Notice the neater lines of color change of the shoe on right.

The diagram below shows the approximate length for each size.

Weave in yarn ends to the wrong side. The basic shoe is ready to felt—see "Felting" on page 34. After felting, follow instructions in the pattern of your choice for finishing details. Lastly, make leather soles for your little shoes, as described in "Soles" on page 37. (If this is a practice shoe, you may decide to skip the leather soles.)

Shoe lengths before felting

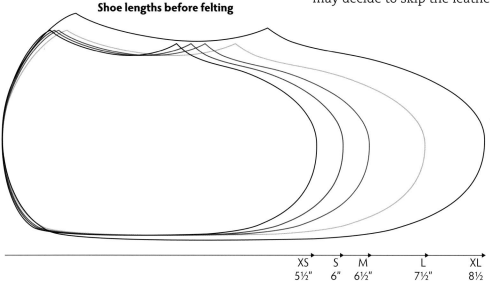

XS	S	M	L	XL
5½"	6"	6½"	7½"	8½

fresh watermelon

Life should be a picnic! These shoes are like luscious slices of seeded pink melon, and will have your little one looking and feeling summery-sweet and mellow. The cool green rind at the base and frothy ruffle at the top give these little shoes a bit of party style—anyone for croquet?

Sizes

XS (S, M, L, XL)

To fit: 0–3 (3–6, 6–12, 12–18, 18–24) months

Length before felting: 5½ (6, 6½, 7½, 8½)"

Length after felting: 3¾ (4¼, 4½, 4¾, 5¼)"

Finished length with leather sole: 4 (4½, 4¾, 5¼, 5¾)"

Gauge

14 dc and 8 rows = 4"

Materials

1 skein *each* of Patons Classic Wool (3.50 oz/100 g; 210 yds/ 192 m)

    A in color 00240 Leaf Green

    B in color 77435 Water Chestnut

    C Approx 3 yds of Patons in color 77532 Cognac Heather, or any dark color, for seeds

Approx 1½ yds, light-pink double-sided ⅜"-wide satin ribbon

Size H-8 (5 mm) crochet hook or size required to obtain gauge

Making the Shoes

Make 2.

Refer to "The Basic Shoe Pattern" on page 7.

Foundation ch: With A, ch 14 (17, 20, 23, 26), pinch, ch 3—17 (20, 23, 26, 29) sts.

Row 1: Dc 1 in 4th ch from hook, 1 dc in next 12 (15, 18, 21, 24) ch, 7 dc in last ch, working down other side of ch, 13 (16, 19, 22, 25) dc—33 (39, 45, 51, 57) sts. Join with sl st to top of ch 3.

Row 2: Ch 3, turn, 1 dc in same st as ch 3, 13 (16, 19, 22, 25) dc, 2 dc in *each* next 7 sts, 12 (15, 18, 21, 24) dc, 2 dc in last st—42 (48, 54, 60, 66) sts. Join with sl st to top of ch 3.

Sizes XS and S only

Row 3: Ch 3, turn, 42 (48) dc—42 (48) sts. With B, join with sl st to top of ch 3.

Row 4: Ch 3, turn, 16 (19) dc, dc2tog 5 times, 16 (19) dc—37 (43) sts. Join with sl st to top of ch 3.

Row 5: Ch 3, turn, 12 (15) dc, dc2tog 7 times, 10 (13) dc, 2 dc in last st—31 (37) sts. Join with sl st to top of ch 3.

Row 6: Ch 3, turn, 9 (12) dc, dc2tog 6 times, 8 (11) dc, dc2tog—24 (30) sts. Join with sl st to top of ch 3.

Row 7: Ch 2, turn, 8 (9) sc, sc2tog 4 (6) times, 8 (9) sc—20 (24) sts. Join with sl st to top of ch 2.

Row 8: Ch 2, turn, 20 (24) sc. Join with sl st to top of ch 2.

Row 9: *Ch 4, sk 2 sts, 1 sc*; rep from * to * 5 (6) more times, ch 4, join with sl st into 1st ch of 1st loop. This creates 7 (8) loops into which you'll attach ruffles. Fasten off.

Size M only

Row 3: Ch 3, turn, 54 dc—54 sts. Join with sl st to top of ch 3.

Row 4: Ch 3, turn, 22 dc, dc2tog 5 times, 22 dc—49 sts. With B, join with sl st to top of ch 3.

Row 5: Ch 3, turn, 18 dc, dc2tog 7 times, 16 dc, 2 dc in last st—43 sts. Join with sl st to top of ch 3.

Row 6: Ch 3, turn, 14 dc, dc2tog 7 times, 13 dc, dc2tog—35 sts. Join with sl st to top of ch 3.

Row 7: Ch 2, turn, 10 sc, dc2tog 7 times, 8 sc, sc2tog—26 sts. Join with sl st to top of ch 2. (There's an extra space at end of row, which will close up with felting.)

Row 8: Ch 2, turn, 26 sc, join with sl st to top of ch 2.

Row 9: *Ch 4, sk 2 sts, 1 sc*; rep from * to * 6 more times, ch 4, join with sl st into the 1st ch of 1st loop. This creates 8 loops into which you'll attach ruffles. Fasten off.

Sizes L and XL only

Row 3: Ch 3, turn, 60 (66) dc—60 (66) sts. Join with sl st to top of ch 3.

Row 4: Ch 3, turn, 25 (27) dc, dc2tog 5 (6) times, 25 (27) dc—55 (60) sts. Join with sl st to top of ch 3.

Row 5: Ch 3, turn, 21 (23) dc, dc2tog 7 times, 19 (23) dc, 2 (0) dc in last 1 (0) st—49 (53) sts. With B, join with sl st to top of ch 3.

Row 6: Ch 3, turn, 18 (20) dc, dc2tog 6 times, 17 (19) dc, dc2tog—42 (46) sts. Join with sl st to top of ch 3.

Row 7: Ch 2, turn, 15 (16) sc, dc2tog 6 (7) times, 13 (14) sc, sc2tog—35 (38) sts. Join with sl st to top of ch 2.

Row 8: Ch 2, turn, 11 (12) sc, dc2tog 6 (7) times, 10 sc, sc2tog—28 (30) sts. Join with sl st to top of ch 2.

Row 9: Ch 2, turn, 28 (30) sc, join with sl st to top of ch 2.

Row 10: *Ch 4, sk 2 sts, 1 sc*; rep from * to * 7 (8) more times, ch 4, join with sl st into 1st ch of 1st loop. This creates 9 (10) loops into which you'll attach ruffles after felting. Fasten off.

All sizes

See "Which Side Is the Right Side?" on page 10. Turn your shoes to the WS and weave in all ends. Weave yarn A toward A and yarn B toward B. Turn shoes to RS.

STITCHING THE SEEDS

Thread a sharp yarn needle with 2 strands of C, approx 18" long, and knot ends. From inside of shoe, pull needle through and make a lazy daisy stitch (page 45). Return needle to inside of shoe and cont, without knotting, to next seed spot as indicated by dotted lines in diagram above right. Make sure to leave a loose length of yarn between seeds. After stitching last seed, tie small knot inside shoe and leave short tail. Don't weave in tail; it will felt into the fabric. Refer to diagram for quantity

and placement of seeds; actual number may vary depending on shoe size.

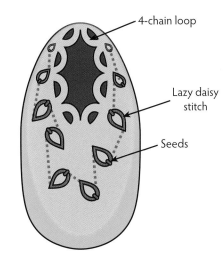

4-chain loop

Lazy daisy stitch

Seeds

Pucker-Free Seeds!

When stitching seeds, place two or three fingers together against the inside of the shoe between seeds. As you move from finishing one seed to beg of next, carry the yarn over your fingers (your fingers are between the shoe and the yarn on the inside). When you pull out your fingers, there will be some loose yarn between seeds. This will shrink and absorb into the shoe as it felts, leaving no puckers and minimal knotting. If excess yarn remains after felting, trim it away.

Felting to Size

Refer to "Felting" on page 34 for complete instructions. Refer to "Sole Patterns" on page 46, as they are the perfect sizing guide during the felting process.

Applying Finishing Stitches

Using a crochet hook, open up the 7 (8, 8, 9, 10) 4-ch loops around top of shoe that closed up during felting. Using yarn B and crochet hook, make a slip knot. Beg at back of shoe and insert hook into first felted loop to left. Ch 6, *1 sc into loop, ch 6*, rep from * to * 1 time. Move to next felted loop, rep from * to * twice until you've worked all the way around felted loops at top of shoe, 1 sc into beg felted loop. Fasten off and weave in ends.

Thread ribbon into darning needle. Do not knot ribbon. Insert needle slightly to right of top front of shoe, just below final (topmost) row of sc. Weave ribbon in and out around shoe between sts until you arrive just left of front of shoe, where you bring needle out. Tie ribbon in a pretty bow.

Adding the Soles

Make and attach leather soles, referring to "Soles" on page 37 for complete instructions.

froggy

Ribbit, ribbit! These little froggies are as green as springtime and will make little feet go hop, hop, hop! With bulbous yellow-green eyes, they're on the lookout for adventures with a lucky boy or girl. Perhaps we'll play on the lily pads in the old mill pond . . . or is it the perfect day to climb on the grapevine?

Sizes

XS (S, M, L, XL)

To fit: 0–3 (3–6, 6–12, 12–18, 18–24) months

Length before felting: 5½ (6, 6½, 7½, 8½)"

Length after felting: 3¾ (4¼, 4½, 4¾, 5¼)"

Finished length with leather sole: 4 (4½, 4¾, 5¼, 5¾)"

Gauge

14 dc and 8 rows = 4"

Materials

1 skein *each* of Patons Classic Wool (3.50 oz/100 g; 210 yds/ 192 m)

    A in color 00240 Leaf Green

    B in color 77223 Lemon Green

1 yd of black in medium worsted-weight yarn, *OR* 3 yds of black in lighter-weight yarn or embroidery floss, for eyes

Size H-8 (5 mm) crochet hook or size required to obtain gauge

Making the Shoes

Make 2.

Refer to "The Basic Shoe Pattern" on page 7.

Foundation ch: With A, ch 14 (17, 20, 23, 26), pinch, ch 3—17 (20, 23, 26, 29) sts.

Row 1: Dc 1 in 4th ch from hook, 1 dc in next 12 (15, 18, 21, 24) ch, 7 dc in last ch, working along other side of ch, 13 (16, 19, 22, 25) dc—33 (39, 45, 51, 57) sts. Join with sl st to top of ch 3.

Row 2: Ch 3, turn, 1 dc in same st as ch 3, 13 (16, 19, 22, 25) dc, 2 dc in *each* of next 7 sts, 12 (15, 18, 21, 24) dc, 2 dc in last st—42 (48, 54, 60, 66) sts. Join with sl st to top of ch 3.

Row 3: Ch 3, turn, 42 (48, 54, 60, 66) dc—42 (48, 54, 60, 66) sts. Join with sl st to top of ch 3.

Row 4: Ch 3, turn, 16 (19, 22, 25, 27) dc, dc2tog 5 (5, 5, 5, 6) times, 16 (19, 22, 25, 27) dc—37 (43, 49, 55, 60) sts. Join with sl st to top of ch 3.

Row 5: Ch 3, turn, 12 (15, 18, 21, 23) dc, dc2tog 7 times, 10 (13, 16, 19, 23) dc, 2 (2, 2, 2, 0) dc in last 1 (1, 1, 1, 0) st—31 (37, 43, 49, 53) sts. Join with sl st to top of ch 3.

Row 6: Ch 3, turn, 9 (12, 14, 18, 20) dc, dc2tog 6 (6, 7, 6, 6) times, 8 (11, 13, 17, 19) dc, dc2tog—24 (30, 35, 42, 46) sts. Join with sl st to top of ch 3.

Sizes XS and S only

Row 7: Ch 2, turn, 8 (9) sc, sc2tog 4 (6) times, 8 (9) sc—20 (24) sts. With B, join with sl st to top of ch 2.

Row 8: Ch 2, turn, 20 (24) sc; with A, join with sl st to top of ch 2.

Row 9: Ch 2, turn, 20 (24) sc, join with sl st to top of ch 2. Fasten off.

Size M only

Row 7: Ch 2, turn, 10 sc, dc2tog 7 times, 8 sc, sc2tog. (26 sts) With B, join with sl st to top of ch 2. (There's an extra space at end of row, which will close up during felting.)

Row 8: Ch 2, turn, 26 sc; with A, join with sl st to top of ch 2.

Row 9: Ch 2, turn, 26 sc, join with sl st to top of ch 2. Fasten off.

Sizes L and XL only

Row 7: Ch 2, turn, 15 (16) sc, dc2tog 6 (7) times, 13 (14) sc, sc2tog—35 (38) sts. Join with sl st to top of ch 2.

Row 8: Ch 2, turn, 11 (12) sc, dc2tog 6 (7) times, 10 sc, sc2tog—28 (30) sts. With B, join with sl st to top of ch 2.

Row 9: Ch 2, turn, 28 (30) sc; with A, join with sl st to top of ch 2.

Row 10: Ch 2, turn, 28 (30) sc, join with sl st to top of ch 2. Fasten off.

All sizes

See "Which Side Is the Right Side?" on page 10. Turn your shoes to the WS and weave in all ends. Weave yarn A toward A and yarn B toward B. Turn shoes to RS.

Making the Eyes

Make 4 rosettes.

Using A, beg with an adjustable ring (see page 43), ch 4, 6 dc in ring; with B, 8 dc in ring—14 dc. Join with sl st to top of ch 4. Fasten off with long outer tail for sewing. Draw center ring closed. With darning needle, pick up edge loop from each dc. Pull slightly on yarn to create a bulge.

Using straight pins, position eyes on both shoes, tucking center yarn tail behind eyes. Make sure placement matches on both shoes. Sew eyes onto faces with hemstitch (page 46), using yarn tail. Weave in ends.

Felting to Size

Refer to "Felting" on page 34 for complete instructions. Refer to "Sole Patterns" on page 46, as they are the perfect sizing guide during the felting process.

Applying Finishing Stitches

See "Basic Embroidery Stitches for Finishing" on page 44. Using 2 strands of medium worsted-weight yarn, embroider details on little shoes. Use 3 or 4 strands if using lighter-weight yarn or embroidery floss.

Eyes: For eye slits, thread needle with black yarn and starting in back of eye patch, bring needle out in center of eye patch A, insert back into shoe B, bring back out at A, insert into shoe at C, and bring out once again at A. Make French knot (page 46) in

center of eye slit for pupil. Secure yarn inside shoe and weave in ends. Rep for second eye.

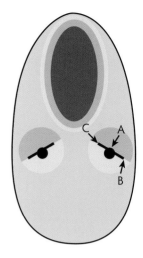

Adding the Soles

Make and attach leather soles, referring to "Soles" on page 37 for complete instructions.

ladybug

Ladybug, ladybug, fly away home! This brightly colored Ladybug is busy and friendly, a charming garden helper that everyone loves to see. Red and black are favorite colors of the infant and toddler set, and polka dots are always chic! Ladybug's face is highlighted by her contrasting antennae and eyes.

Sizes

XS (S, M, L, XL)

To fit: 0–3 (3–6, 6–12, 12–18, 18–24) months

Length before felting: 5½ (6, 6½, 7½, 8½)"

Length after felting: 3¾ (4¼, 4½, 4¾, 5¼)"

Finished length, with leather sole: 4 (4½, 4¾, 5¼, 5¾)"

Gauge

14 dc and 8 rows = 4"

Materials

1 skein *each* of Patons Classic Wool (3.50 oz/100 g; 210 yds/ 192 m)

   A in color 00250 Bright Red

   B in color 00226 Black

1 yd *each* of bright-green and gold or silver metallic in medium worsted-weight yarn, OR 3 yds *each* of bright-green and gold or silver metallic in lighter-weight yarn or embroidery floss, for eyes and antennae

Size H-8 (5 mm) crochet hook or size required to obtain gauge

White chalk marker

Making the Shoes

Make 2.

Refer to "The Basic Shoe Pattern" on page 7.

Foundation ch: With A, ch 14 (17, 20, 23, 26), pinch, ch 3—17 (20, 23, 26, 29) sts.

Row 1: Dc 1 in 4th ch from hook, 1 dc in next 12 (15, 18, 21, 24) ch, 7 dc in last ch, working down other side of ch, 13 (16, 19, 22, 25) dc—33 (39, 45, 51, 57) sts. Join with sl st to top of ch 3.

Row 2: Ch 3, turn, 1 dc in same st as ch 3, 13 (16, 19, 22, 25) dc, 2 dc in *each* of next 7 sts, 12 (15, 18, 21, 24) dc, 2 dc in last st—42 (48, 54, 60, 66) sts. Join with sl st to top of ch 3.

Row 3: Ch 3, turn, 14 (16, 18, 21, 23) dc; with B, 14 (16, 18, 18, 20) dc; with A, 14 (16, 18, 21, 23) dc—42 (48, 54, 60, 66) sts. Join with sl st to top of ch 3.

Row 4: Ch 3, turn, 14 (16, 18, 21, 23) dc; with B, 2 (3, 4, 4, 4) dc, dc2tog 5 (5, 5, 5, 6) times, 2 (3, 4, 4, 4) dc; with A, 14 (16, 18, 21, 23) dc—37 (43, 49, 55, 60) sts. Join with sl st to top of ch 3.

Dc2tog Color Change

A color change in the middle of the dc2tog is necessary in sizes M, L, and XL to make a smooth outline of Ladybug's head. This dc2tog color change is slightly different from the standard dc2tog. See page 43 on how to make a color change between the two stitches when making the decrease.

Sizes XS and S only

Row 5: Ch 3, turn, 12 (15) dc, dc2tog; with B, dc2tog 4 (5) times; with A, dc2tog 2 (1) times, 10 (13) dc, 2 dc in last st—31 (37) sts. Join with sl st to top of ch 3.

Row 6: Ch 3, turn, 9 (12) dc, dc2tog 6 times, 8 (11) dc, dc2tog—24 (30) sts. Join with sl st to top of ch 3.

Row 7: Ch 2, turn, 8 (9) sc, sc2tog 4 (6) times, 8 (9) sc—20 (24) sts. Join with sl st to top of ch 2.

Row 8: Ch 2, turn, 20 (24) sc; with B, join with sl st to top of ch 2.

Row 9: Ch 2, turn, 20 (24) sc, join with sl st to top of ch 2. Fasten off.

Size M only

Row 5: Ch 3, turn, 18 dc; with B, dc2tog 6 times; with A, dc2tog, 16 dc, 2 dc in last st—43 sts. Join with sl st to top of ch 3.

Row 6: Ch 3, turn, 14 dc, dc2tog 2 times, dc2tog color change to B, dc2tog 2 times, dc2tog color change to A, dc2tog, 13 dc, dc2tog—35 sts. Join with sl st to top of ch 3.

Row 7: Ch 2, turn, 10 sc, dc2tog 7 times, 8 sc, sc2tog—26 sts. Join with sl st to top of ch 2. (There's an extra space at the end of the row, which will close up with felting.)

Row 8: Ch 2, turn, 26 sc; with B, join with sl st to top of ch 2.

Row 9: Ch 2, turn, 26 sc, join with sl st to top of ch 2. Fasten off.

Row 5: Ch 3, turn, 21 (23) dc; with B, dc2tog 6 (7) times, dc2tog color change to A 1 (0) time; 19 (23) dc, 2 (0) dc in last 1 (0) st—49 (53) sts. Join with sl st to top of ch 3.

Row 6: Ch 3, turn, 18 (20) dc, dc2tog; with B, dc2tog 4 times; with A, dc2tog, 17 (19) dc, dc2tog—42 (46) sts. Join with sl st to top of ch 3.

Row 7: Ch 2, turn, 15 (16) sc, dc2tog 6 (7) times, 13 (14) sc, sc2tog—35 (38) sts. Join with sl st to top of ch 2.

Row 8: Ch 2, turn, 11 (12) sc, dc2tog 6 (7) times, 10 sc, sc2tog—28 (30) sts. Join with sl st to top of ch 2.

Row 9: Ch 2, turn, 28 (30) sc; with B, join with sl st to top of ch 2.

Row 10: Ch 2, turn, 28 (30) sc, join with sl st to top of ch 2. Fasten off.

All sizes

See "Which Side Is the Right Side?" on page 10. Turn your shoes to the WS and weave in all ends. Weave A toward A and B toward B. Turn shoes to RS.

Adding the Polka Dots

Make 10 (12, 12, 14, 16) rosettes.

Using B, make adjustable ring (see page 43), ch 3, 6 sc in ring, join with sl st to top of ch 3.

Fasten off, leaving a long tail for sewing. Draw ring closed.

Using straight pins, position polka dots randomly on both shoes, tucking center yarn tail behind the dots. Thread darning needle with tail of polka dot, and sew polka dot onto shoe with hemstitch (page 46). Rep with rem polka dots. Weave in ends.

Felting to Size

Refer to "Felting" on page 34 for complete instructions. Refer to "Sole Patterns" (page 46), as they are the perfect sizing guide during the felting process.

Applying Finishing Stitches

Refer to "Basic Embroidery Stitches for Finishing" on page 44. Use 1 strand of medium worsted-weight yarn to embroider details on little shoes. Use 2 or 3 strands if using lighter-weight yarn or embroidery floss.

See "Make a Face Stencil" on page 44. Using chalk or white pencil, mark the eyes and antennae on Ladybug's face using the stencil. Use straight pins to mark eyes on both shoes.

Eyes: Using a sharp yarn needle and green yarn, make French knot (page 46) at eye position. Secure inside shoe. Weave in ends. Rep for second eye.

Antennae: Using sharp needle and metallic yarn, chain stitch (page 45) antennae lines. Secure ends inside shoe, and weave in tails.

Adding the Soles

Make and attach leather soles, referring to "Soles" on page 37 for complete instructions.

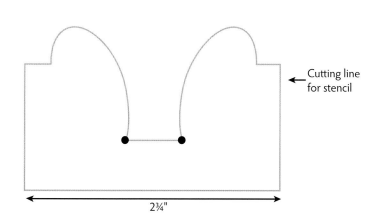

Cutting line for stencil

2¾"

ollie owl

Whooo is Ollie? Ollie is the most optimistic, outgoing, and observant of all owls. He is occasionally odd, but never obnoxious or obstinate, and he is quite open-minded. He is as happy to be out and about in the daytime as in the night. Some special girl or boy will have a real hoot wearing these offbeat ocular booties. Ollie's face is crocheted separately and sewn on before felting, giving him a more three-dimensional visage.

Sizes

XS (S, M, L, XL)

To fit: 0–3 (3–6, 6–12, 12–18, 18–24) months

Length before felting: 5½ (6, 6½, 7½, 8½)"

Length after felting: 3¾ (4¼, 4½, 4¾, 5¼)"

Finished length, with leather sole: 4 (4½, 4¾, 5¼, 5¾)"

Gauge

14 dc and 8 rows = 4"

Materials

1 skein *each* of Patons Classic Wool (3.50 oz/100 g; 210 yds/ 192 m)

    A in color 00227 Taupe

    B in color 00229 Natural Mix

    C in color 77615 Yellow

    D in color 00201 Winter White

    E in color 77010 Natural Marl

1 yd of black in medium worsted-weight yarn, OR 3 yds of black in lighter-weight yarn or embroidery floss, for eyes and beak

Size H-8 (5 mm) crochet hook or size required to obtain gauge

Making the Shoes

Make 2.

Refer to "The Basic Shoe Pattern" on page 7.

Foundation ch: With A, ch 14 (17, 20, 23, 26), pinch, ch 3—17 (20, 23, 26, 29) sts.

Row 1: Dc 1 in 4th ch from hook, 1 dc in next 12 (15, 18, 21, 24) ch, 7 dc in last ch, working other side of ch, 13 (16, 19, 22, 25) dc—33 (39, 45, 51, 57) sts. Join with sl st to top of ch 3.

Row 2: Ch 3, turn, 1 dc in same st as ch 3, 13 (16, 19, 22, 25) dc, 2 dc in *each* of next 7 sts, 12 (15, 18, 21, 24) dc, 2 dc in last st—42 (48, 54, 60, 66) sts. Join with sl st to top of ch 3.

Row 3: Ch 3, turn, 14 (16, 18, 21, 23) dc; with B, 14 (16, 18, 18, 20) dc; with A, 14 (16, 18, 21, 23) dc—42 (48, 54, 60, 66) sts. Join with sl st to top of ch 3.

Row 4: Ch 3, turn, 14 (16, 18, 21, 23) dc; with B, 2 (3, 4, 4, 4) dc, dc2tog 5 (5, 5, 5, 6) times, 2 (3, 4, 4, 4) dc; with A, 14 (16, 18, 21, 23) dc—37 (43, 49, 55, 60) sts. Join with sl st to top of ch 3.

See page 43 on how to make a color change between the two stitches when making the decrease.

Dc2tog Color Change

A color change in the middle of the dc2tog is necessary in sizes M, L, and XL to make a smooth outline of Ollie Owl's head. This dc2tog color change is slightly different from the standard dc2tog. See page 43 on how to make a color change between the two stitches when making the decrease.

Sizes XS and S only

Row 5: Ch 3, turn, 12 (15) dc, dc2tog; with B, dc2tog 4 (5) times; with A, dc2tog 2 (1) times, 10 (13) dc, 2 dc in last st—31 (37) sts. Join with sl st to top of ch 3.

Row 6: Ch 3, turn, 9 (12) dc, dc2tog 6 times, 8 (11) dc, dc2tog—24 (30) sts. Join with sl st to top of ch 3.

Row 7: Ch 2, turn, 8 (9) sc, sc2tog 4 (6) times, 8 (9) sc—20 (24) sts. Join with sl st to top of ch 2.

Row 8: Ch 2, turn, 20 (24) sc, join with sl st to top of ch 2.

Row 9: Ch 2, turn, 20 (24) sc, join with sl st to top of ch 2. Fasten off.

Size M only

Row 5: Ch 3, turn, 18 dc; with B, dc2tog 6 times; with A, dc2tog, 16 dc, 2 dc in last st—43 sts. Join with sl st to top of ch 3.

Row 6: Ch 3, turn, 14 dc, dc2tog 2 times, dc2tog color change to B, dc2tog 2 times, dc2tog color change to A, dc2tog, 13 dc, dc2tog—35 sts. Join with sl st to top of ch 3.

Row 7: Ch 2, turn, 10 sc, dc2tog 7 times, 8 sc, sc2tog—26 sts. Join with sl st to top of ch 2. (There's an extra space at end of row, which will close up with felting.)

Row 8: Ch 2, turn, 26 sc, join with sl st to top of ch 2.

Row 9: Ch 2, turn, 26 sc, join with sl st to top of ch 2. Fasten off

Sizes L and XL only

Row 5: Ch 3, turn, 21 (23) dc; with B, dc2tog 6 (7) times, dc2tog color change to A 1 (0) time; with A, 19 (23) dc, 2 (0) dc in last 1 (0) st—49 (53) sts. Join with sl st to top of ch 3.

Row 6: Ch 3, turn, 18 (20) dc, dc2tog; with B, dc2tog 4 (4) times; with A, dc2tog 17 (19) dc, dc2tog—42 (46) sts. Join with sl st to top of ch 3.

Row 7: Ch 2, turn, 15 (16) dc, dc2tog 6 (7) times, 13 (14) dc, sc2tog—35 (38) sts. Join with sl st to top of ch 2.

Row 8: Ch 2, turn, 11 (12) sc, dc2tog 6 (7) times, 10 sc, sc2tog—28 (30) sts. Join with sl st to top of ch 2.

Row 9: Ch 2, turn, 28 (30) sc, join with sl st to top of ch 2.

Row 10: Ch 2, turn, 28 (30) sc, join with sl st to top of ch 2. Fasten off.

All sizes

See "Which Side Is the Right Side?" on page 10. Turn your shoes to the WS and weave in all ends. Weave A toward A and B toward B. Turn shoes to RS.

Making the Face Mask

Make 1 for each shoe.

Row 1 (irises of eyes): Using C, make adjustable ring (page 43), ch 3, 6 sc in ring, join with sl st to top of ch 3. Fasten off with short tail. Rep to make second rosette. Pull ring tight to close gap in middle.

Row 2 (facial disc): Using D, make a slip knot, insert hook into first st next to joining sl st, pull slip knot through, ch 2, 2 sc in *each* of next 6 sts, 1 sc back into first st, sl st to top of ch 2. Join two rosettes by inserting hook into second rosette next to its joining sl st, 2 sc in *each* of next 7 sts; with C, join with sl st to first sc. Ch 1, turn.

Row 3 (face rim feathers): On RS, starting in next st from ch and using E, *1 sc, 2 sc*; rep from * to * 6 times. Move onto other eye, into second st from sl st, rep from * to * 6 times, join with sl st to ch 1. Fasten off with long tail for sewing. This row establishes RS of face mask.

Ear tufts: On RS, *beg at center of face mask, count 8 sts to right. Using B, make a slip knot, insert hook, pull slip knot through, ch 3, dc2tog. Fasten off, leaving 2" tail. Do not weave in;

tail will felt into ear tuft and be trimmed later.* Turn face mask over and rep from * to *.

Ear Tuft
Ch 3, dc2tog, starting in 8th st from center.

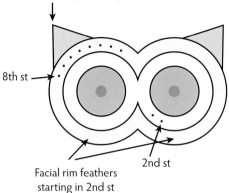

8th st

Facial rim feathers starting in 2nd st

2nd st

Pull all yarn tails to WS and trim to tuck behind mask, leaving long tail from row 3 for sewing. Using straight pins, position face masks on shoes, making certain that placement is same on both shoes. Using yarn tail and running stitch (page 46), sew face mask on broken stitching line as shown. Sew face mask around eyes, with a few sts going up ear tufts, instead of around outer edge, to provide extra dimension in face after felting. Weave in ends.

Line of running stitch

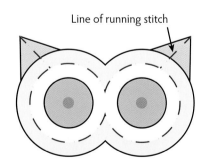

Felting to Size

Refer to "Felting" (page 34) for complete instructions. Refer to "Sole Patterns" on page 46, as they are the perfect sizing guide during the felting process.

After felting, but before shoes are dry, accentuate the ear tufts by pulling on the felted yarn tails. Trim them with scissors to look like feathery points.

Applying Finishing Stitches

See "Basic Embroidery Stitches for Finishing" on page 44. Use 1 strand of medium worsted-weight yarn to embroider details on little shoes. Use 2 or 3 strands if you are using lighter-weight yarn or embroidery floss.

Eyes and beak: To minimize knots and weaving inside shoes, use 1 long strand of yarn to embroider eyes and beak. Keep yarn that runs between eyes and beak between layers of wool, so there will be no strings inside to catch baby's foot. Using sharp yarn needle and black yarn with a small knot and a tail to weave in, come from the inside of shoe and make French knot (page 46) in center of one yellow iris. Carry yarn between layers of face mask and actual shoe, and make French knot for second eye. Staying between felted layers, bring yarn out at bottom center of white facial discs, and make 3 vertical ½"-long satin sts (page 46), working

downward over the face rim feathers and using same 2 holes. Secure end inside shoe and weave in tails.

Adding the Soles

Make and attach leather soles, referring to "Soles" on page 37 for complete instructions.

panda bear

Who is black and white and cute all over? Baby Panda Bear peeks from the bamboo grove. She may look silly with her giant dark eyes on her moon-white face, but she is a gentle and loyal playmate who will keep all of your dearest secrets while you wear these little shoes.

Sizes

XS (S, M, L, XL)

To fit: 0–3 (3–6, 6–12, 12–18, 18–24) months

Length before felting: 5½ (6, 6½, 7½, 8½)"

Length after felting: 3¾ (4¼, 4½, 4¾, 5¼)"

Finished length, with leather sole: 4 (4½, 4¾, 5¼, 5¾)"

Gauge

14 dc and 8 rows = 4"

Materials

1 skein *each* of Patons Classic Wool (3.50 oz/100 g; 210 yds/ 192 m)

    A in color 00226 Black

    B in color 00201 Winter White

1 yd *each* of blue and pink in medium worsted-weight yarn, *OR* 3 yds *each* of blue and pink in lighter-weight yarn or embroidery floss, for eyes and nose

Size H-8 (5 mm) crochet hook or size required to obtain gauge

Making the Shoes

Make 2.

Refer to "The Basic Shoe Pattern" on page 7.

Foundation ch: With A, make a slip knot, ch 14 (17, 20, 23, 26), pinch, ch 3—17 (20, 23, 26, 29) sts.

Row 1: Dc 1 in 4th ch from hook, 1 dc in next 12 (15, 18, 21, 24) ch, 7 dc in last ch, working down other side of ch, 13 (16, 19, 22, 25) dc—33 (39, 45, 51, 57) sts. Join with sl st to top of ch 3.

Row 2: Ch 3, turn, 1 dc in same st as ch 3, 13 (16, 19, 22, 25) dc, 2 dc in *each* of next 7 sts, 12 (15, 18, 21, 24) dc, 2 dc in last st—42 (48, 54, 60, 66) sts. Join with sl st to top of ch 3.

Row 3: Ch 3, turn, 9 (12, 15, 18, 21) dc; with B, 24 dc; with A, 9 (12, 15, 18, 21) dc—42 (48, 54, 60, 66) sts. Join with sl st to top of ch 3.

Row 4: Ch 3, turn, 9 (12, 15, 18, 21) dc; with B, 7 (7, 7, 7, 6) dc, dc2tog 5 (5, 5, 5, 6) times, 7 (7, 7, 7, 6) dc; with A, 9 (12, 15, 18, 21) dc—37 (43, 49, 55, 60) sts. Join with sl st to top of ch 3.

Row 5: Ch 3, turn, 9 (12, 15, 18, 21) dc; with B, 3 (3, 3, 3, 2) dc, dc2tog 7 times, 2 dc; with A, 8 (11, 14, 17, 21) dc, 2 (2, 2, 2, 0) dc in last 1 (1, 1, 1, 0) st—31 (37, 43, 49, 53) sts. Join with sl st to top of ch 3.

Row 6: Ch 3, turn, 9 (12, 14, 18, 20) dc, dc2tog; with B, dc2tog 5 (5, 6, 5, 5) times; with A, 8 (11, 13, 17, 19) dc, dc2tog—24 (30, 35, 42, 46) sts. Join with sl st to top of ch 3.

Sizes XS and S only

Row 7: Ch 2, turn, 8 (9) sc, sc2tog 4 (6) times, 8 (9) sc—20 (24) sts. Join with sl st to top of ch 2.

Row 8: Ch 2, turn, 20 (24) sc, join with sl st to top of ch 2.

Row 9: Ch 2, turn, 20 (24) sc, join with sl st to top of ch 2. Fasten off.

Size M only

Row 7: Ch 2, turn, 10 sc, dc2tog 7 times, 8 sc, sc2tog—26 sts. Join with sl st to top of ch 2. (There will be an extra space at end of row, which will close up with felting.)

Row 8: Ch 2, turn, 26 sc, join with sl st to top of ch 2.

Row 9: Ch 2, turn, 26 sc, join with sl st to top of ch 2. Fasten off.

Sizes L and XL only

Row 7: Ch 2, turn, 15 (16) sc, dc2tog 6 (7) times, 13 (14) sc, sc2tog—35 (38) sts. Join with sl st to top of ch 2.

Row 8: Ch 2, turn, 11 (12) sc, dc2tog 6 (7) times, 10 sc, sc2tog—28 (30) sts. Join with sl st to top of ch 2.

Row 9: Ch 2, turn, 28 (30) sc. Join with sl st to top of ch 2.

Row 10: Ch 2, turn, 28 (30) sc. Join with sl st to top of ch 2. Fasten off.

All sizes

See "Which Side Is the Right Side?" on page 10. Turn your shoes to the WS and weave in all ends. Weave yarn A toward A and yarn B toward B. Turn shoes to RS.

EARS

Make 4 half-rosettes.

Using A, make adjustable ring (page 43), ch 3, 5 sc in ring, ch 2, turn, 2 sc in *each* of next 5 sts. Draw center ring closed. Fasten off with long outer tail for sewing.

Weave in center tail. Pin ears to face as shown below, RS down. Make sure placement matches on both shoes. Sew onto faces with hemstitch (page 46) using yarn tail. Weave in ends. Tug ears to be sure they are secure and upright.

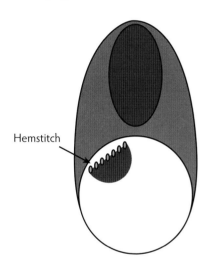

Hemstitch

EYE PATCHES

Make 4 ovals.

Using A, ch 3, work 1 sc, 2 dc, 2 sc, 2 dc, 1 sc in first ch. Join with sl st to top of ch 3. Fasten off, leaving long tail for sewing. Position eye patches on both shoes, tucking inner tails behind eye patch and making sure placement matches. Sew eye patches onto faces with hemstitch using yarn tail. Weave in ends.

Felting to Size

Refer to "Felting" (page 34) for complete instructions. Refer to "Sole Patterns" on page 46, as they are the perfect sizing guide during the felting process. Before drying, straighten ears. If you encounter a stubborn ear, pin loosely into position with a safety pin and allow to dry.

Applying Finishing Stitches

See "Basic Embroidery Stitches for Finishing" on page 44. Use 1 strand of medium worsted-weight yarn to embroider details on little shoes. Use 2 or 3 strands if you are using lighter-weight yarn or embroidery floss.

See "Make a Face Stencil" on page 44. Use straight pins to mark eyes on both shoes. Mark a nose and mouth on both shoes using the stencil.

Eyes: Using sharp yarn needle and blue yarn, make French knot (page 46) at eye position. Secure inside shoe. Weave in ends. Rep for second eye.

Nose: Using sharp yarn needle and pink yarn, bring needle out at point A and in at point B, as indicated on stencil. Rep, making shorter lines of stitching below first line, to make a triangle (3 sts should do it). Secure inside shoe and weave in ends.

Mouth: With sharp yarn needle and black yarn, bring needle out at point C, insert at point D, out at point E, in at D, out at F, and in at D. Secure inside shoe and weave in ends.

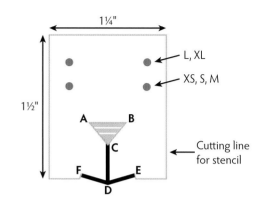

Adding the Soles

Make and attach leather soles, referring to "Soles" on page 37 for complete instructions.

silly monkey

*T*his Silly Monkey is reminiscent of the red-heel sock monkey our grandmas made for us. What was once created for the feet became an iconic playmate, and now that little buddy wants to get back on some feet! Is Silly Monkey right for you? Do you like giggles and mischief and all-day fun? Silly Monkey loves the jungle gym, and he might try to steal your banana!

Sizes

XS (S, M, L, XL)

To fit: 0–3 (3–6, 6–12, 12–18, 18–24) months

Length before felting: 5½ (6, 6½, 7½, 8½)"

Length after felting: 3¾ (4¼, 4½, 4¾, 5¼)"

Finished length, with leather sole: 4 (4½, 4¾, 5¼, 5¾)"

Gauge

14 dc and 8 rows = 4"

Materials

1 skein *each* of Patons Classic Wool (3.50 oz/100 g; 210 yds/ 192 m)

    A in color 77251 Light Gray Marl

    B in color 00201 Winter White

    C in color 00230 Bright Red

1 yd of black in medium worsted-weight yarn, OR 3 yds of black in lighter-weight yarn or embroidery floss, for eyes and mouth

Size H-8 (5 mm) crochet hook or size required to obtain gauge

Making the Shoes

Make 2.

Refer to "The Basic Shoe Pattern" on page 7.

Foundation ch: With A, make a slip knot, ch 14 (17, 20, 23, 26), pinch, ch 3—17 (20, 23, 26, 29) sts.

Row 1: Dc 1 in 4th ch from hook, 1 dc in next 12 (15, 18, 21, 24) ch, 7 dc in last ch, working down other side of ch, 13 (16, 19, 22, 25) dc—33 (39, 45, 51, 57) sts. Join with sl st to top of ch 3.

Row 2: Ch 3, turn, 1 dc in same st as ch 3, 13 (16, 19, 22, 25) dc, 2 dc in *each* of next 7 sts, 12 (15, 18, 21, 24) dc, 2 dc in last st—42 (48, 54, 60, 66) sts. Join with sl st to top of ch 3.

Row 3: Ch 3, turn, 14 (16, 18, 21, 23) dc; with B, 14 (16, 18, 18, 20) dc; with A, 14 (16, 18, 21, 23) dc—42 (48, 54, 60, 66) sts. Join with sl st to top of ch 3.

Row 4: Ch 3, turn, 14 (16, 18, 21, 23) dc; with B, 2 (3, 4, 4, 4) dc; with C, 5 (5, 5, 5, 6) dc; with B, 2 (3, 4, 4, 4) dc; with A, 14 (16, 18, 21, 23) dc—37 (43, 49, 55, 60) sts. Join with sl st to top of ch 3.

Sizes XS and S only

Row 5: Ch 3, turn, 12 (15) dc, dc2tog; with B, 4 (5) dc; with A, dc2tog 2 (1) times, 10 (13) dc, 2 dc in last st—31 (37) sts. Join with sl st to top of ch 3.

Row 6: Ch 3, turn, 9 (12) dc, dc2tog 6 times, 8 (11) dc, dc2tog—24 (30) sts. Join with sl st to top of ch 3.

Row 7: Ch 2, turn, 8 (9) sc, sc2tog 4 (6) times, 8 (9) sc—20 (24) sts. With B, join with sl st to top of ch 2.

Row 8: Ch 2, turn, 20 (24) sc; with C, join with sl st to top of ch 2.

Row 9: Ch 2, turn, 20 (24) sc, join with sl st to top of ch 2. Fasten off.

Size M only

Row 5: Ch 3, turn, 18 dc; with B, dc2tog 6 times; with A, dc2tog, 16 dc, 2 dc in last st—43 sts. Join with sl st to top of ch 3.

Row 6: Ch 3, turn, 14 dc, dc2tog 7 times, 13 dc, dc2tog—35 sts. Join with sl st to top of ch 3.

Row 7: Ch 2, turn, 10 sc, dc2tog 7 times, 8 sc, sc2tog—26 sts. With B, join with sl st to top of ch 2. (There's an extra space at end of row, which will close up with felting.)

Row 8: Ch 2, turn, 26 sc; with C, join with sl st to top of ch 2.

Row 9: Ch 2, turn, 26 sc, join with sl st to top of ch 2. Fasten off.

Sizes L and XL only

Row 5: Ch 3, turn, 21 (23) dc; with B, dc2tog 6 (7) times; with A, 20 (23) dc, 2 (0) dc in last 1 (0) st—49 (53) sts. Join with sl st to top of ch 3.

Row 6: Ch 3, turn, 18 (20) dc, dc2tog 6 times, 17 (19) dc, dc2tog—42 (46) sts. Join with sl st to top of ch 3.

Row 7: Ch 2, turn, 15 (16) sc, dc2tog 6 (7) times, 13 (14) sc, sc2tog—35 (38) sts. Join with sl st to top of ch 2.

Row 8: Ch 2, turn, 11 (12) sc, dc2tog 6 (7) times, 10 sc, sc2tog—28 (30) sts. With B, join with sl st to top of ch 2.

Row 9: Ch 2, turn, 28 (30) sc; with C, join with sl st to top of ch 2.

Row 10: Ch 2, turn, 28 (30) sc, join with sl st to top of ch 2. Fasten off.

All sizes

See "Which Side Is the Right Side?" on page 10. Turn your shoes to the WS and weave in all ends. Weave A toward A and B toward B. Turn shoes to RS.

EARS

Make 4 rosettes.

Using A, beg with an adjustable ring (page 43), ch 4 (count as 1 dc), 9 dc in ring—10 sts. Join with sl st to top of ch 4. Draw center ring closed. Fasten off

with long tail for sewing. Weave center tail into ear.

Using straight pins, position ears on both shoes, RS forward. Make sure placement matches on both shoes. Sew ears onto faces with a hemstitch (page 46) using yarn tail. Weave in ends.

Felting to Size

Refer to "Felting" on page 34 for complete instructions. Refer to "Sole Patterns" on page 46, as they are the perfect sizing guide during the felting process.

Applying Finishing Stitches

See "Basic Embroidery Stitches for Finishing" on page 44. Use 1 strand of medium worsted-weight yarn to embroider details on little shoes. Use 2 or 3 strands if you are using lighter-weight yarn or embroidery floss.

Eyes: Make a French knot (page 46). Secure inside shoe. Weave in ends. Rep for second eye.

Mouth: Start at one outside edge of red area and backstitch (page 45) across center to form mouth.

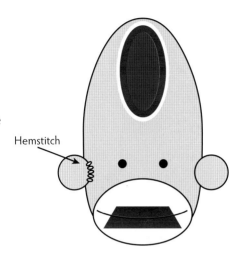

Adding the Soles

Make and attach leather soles, referring to "Soles" on page 37 for complete instructions.

sparky dog

Is that the fire truck's siren you hear? If so, Sparky Dog will be on board! Sparky is a deluxe dalmatian, eager to please and ready to work hard. Sparky can be trusted to take good care of little feet, and she never minds having her ears tugged or spots counted again and again. Wearing these little shoes will be like having your best friend at your heels.

Sizes

XS (S, M, L, XL)

To fit: 0–3 (3–6, 6–12, 12–18, 18–24) months

Length before felting: 5½ (6, 6½, 7½, 8½)"

Length after felting: 3¾ (4¼, 4½, 4¾, 5¼)"

Finished length, with leather sole: 4 (4½, 4¾, 5¼, 5¾)"

Gauge

14 dc and 8 rows = 4"

Materials

1 skein *each* of Patons Classic Wool (3.50 oz/100 g; 210 yds/ 192 m)

> **A** in color 00201 Winter White
>
> **B** in color 00230 Bright Red
>
> **C** in color 00226 Black

2 yds of black in medium worsted-weight yarn, OR 4 yds of black in lighter-weight yarn or embroidery floss, for nose and mouth

1 yd *each* of blue and pink in medium worsted-weight yarn, OR 3 yds *each* of blue and pink in lighter-weight yarn, or embroidery floss, for eyes and tongue

Size H-8 (5 mm) crochet hook or size required to obtain gauge

Making the Shoes

Make 2.

Refer to "The Basic Shoe Pattern" on page 7.

Foundation ch: With A, make a slip knot, ch 14 (17, 20, 23, 26), pinch, ch 3—17 (20, 23, 26, 29) sts.

Row 1: Dc 1 in 4th ch from hook, 1 dc in next 12 (15, 18, 21, 24) ch, 7 dc in last ch, work down other side of ch, 13 (16, 19, 22, 25) dc—33 (39, 45, 51, 57) sts. Join with sl st to top of ch 3.

Row 2: Ch 3, turn, 1 dc in same st as ch 3, 13 (16, 19, 22, 25) dc, 2 dc in *each* of next 7 sts, 12 (15, 18, 21, 24) dc, 2 dc in last st—42 (48, 54, 60, 66) sts. Join with sl st to top of ch 3.

Row 3: Ch 3, turn, 42 (48, 54, 60, 66) dc—42 (48, 54, 60, 66) sts. Join with sl st to top of ch 3.

Row 4: Ch 3, turn, 16 (19, 22, 25, 27) dc, dc2tog 5 (5, 5, 5, 6) times, 16 (19, 22, 25, 27) dc—37 (43, 49, 55, 60) sts. Join with sl st to top of ch 3.

Row 5: Ch 3, turn, 12 (15, 18, 21, 23) dc, dc2tog 7 times, 10 (13, 16, 19, 23) dc, 2 (2, 2, 2, 0) dc in last 1 (1, 1, 1, 0) st—31 (37, 43, 49, 53) sts. Join with sl st to top of ch 3.

Row 6: Ch 3, turn, 9 (12, 14, 18, 20) dc, dc2tog 6 (6, 7, 6, 6) times, 8 (11, 13, 17, 19) dc, dc2tog—24 (30, 35, 42, 46) sts. Join with sl st to top of ch 3.

Sizes XS and S only

Row 7: Ch 2, turn, 8 (9) sc, sc2tog 4 (6) times, 8 (9) sc—20 (24) sts. With B, join with sl st to top of ch 2.

Row 8: Ch 2, turn, 20 (24) sc, join with sl st to top of ch 2.

Row 9: Ch 2, turn, 20 (24) sc, join with sl st to top of ch 2. Fasten off.

Size M only

Row 7: Ch 2, turn, 10 sc, dc2tog 7 times, 8 sc, sc2tog—26 sts. With B, join with sl st to top of ch 2. (There's an extra space at end of row, which will close up with felting.)

Row 8: Ch 2, turn, 26 sc, join with sl st to top of ch 2.

Row 9: Ch 2, turn, 26 sc, join with sl st to top of ch 2. Fasten off.

Sizes L and XL only

Row 7: Ch 2, turn, 15 (16) sc, dc2tog 6 (7) times, 13 (14) sc, sc2tog—35 (38) sts. Join with sl st to top of ch 2.

Row 8: Ch 2, turn, 11 (12) sc, dc2tog 6 (7) times, 10 sc, sc2tog—28 (30) sts. With B, join with sl st to top of ch 2.

Row 9: Ch 2, turn, 28 (30) sc, join with sl st to top of ch 2.

Row 10: Ch 2, turn, 28 (30) sc, join with sl st to top of ch 2. Fasten off.

All sizes

See "Which Side Is the Right Side?" on page 10. Turn your shoes to the WS and weave in all ends. Weave yarn A toward A and yarn B toward B. Turn shoes to RS.

SPOTS

Place pins to mark where spots will go, using the diagram at right as a guide. Thread a sharp yarn needle with 1 strand of C, 18" long, and make a knot with a short tail. Use the diagram as a general guide for distribution and quantity of spots; actual number of spots may vary depending on shoe size. Making short sts will result in round spots. From inside, pull needle through and make a lazy daisy stitch (page 45). Return needle to inside of shoe and continue,

without knotting, to next spot, as indicated by dotted lines in illustration below. Make sure to leave a loose gap of yarn between spots. After stitching last spot, tie a small knot inside shoe and leave a short tail. There is no need to weave in tail end; it will felt into fabric.

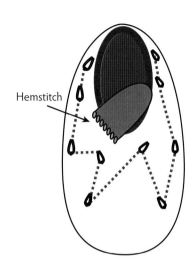

Hemstitch

Pucker-Free Spots!

When stitching spots, place two or three fingers together against the inside of the shoe between spots. As you move from finishing one spot to beg of next, carry the yarn over your fingers (your fingers are between the shoe and the yarn on the inside). When you pull out your fingers, the yarn will be loose between spots. This will shrink and absorb into the shoe as it felts, leaving no puckers and minimal knotting. If excess yarn remains after felting, trim it away.

EARS

Make 2.

Sizes XS, S, and M: Using C, make a slip knot, ch 6, pinch, ch 3. Dc 1 in 4th ch from hook, 1 dc in *each* of next 4 sts, 6 dc in last ch, 5 dc down other side of ch. Fasten off with long tail for sewing.

Sizes L and XL: Using C, make a slip knot, ch 8, pinch, ch 4. Tr 1 in 5th ch from hook, 1 tr in *each* of next 6 sts, 6 tr in last ch, 7 tr down other side of ch. Fasten off with long tail for sewing.

All Sizes: Weave in center tail. Using straight pins, position ears on both shoes. Pin ears upward along bottom edge of red border on either side of face; see diagram on page 33

for ear placement. Make sure placement matches on both shoes. Sew ears onto faces with a hemstitch (page 46) using yarn tail. Weave in ends. Tug ears to be sure they are secure.

Felting to Size

Refer to "Felting" on page 34 for complete instructions. Refer to "Sole Patterns" on page 46, as they are the perfect sizing guide during the felting process. Before drying, smooth or steam out folds or wrinkles on the ears.

Applying Finishing Stitches

See "Basic Embroidery Stitches for Finishing" on page 44. Use 1 strand of medium worsted-weight yarn to embroider details on little shoes. Use 2 or 3 strands if you are using lighter-weight yarn or embroidery floss.

See "Make a Face Stencil" on page 44. Use straight pins to mark eyes on both shoes. Mark nose and mouth on both shoes using the stencil.

Eyes: Using a sharp yarn needle and blue yarn, make a French knot (page 46) at eye position. Secure inside shoe. Weave in ends. Rep for second eye.

Nose: Using a sharp yarn needle and black yarn, bring needle out at point A and in at point B, as indicated on stencil. Rep stitching below, making shorter and shorter lines of stitching, to make a triangle; 3 sts should do it. Secure inside shoe and weave in ends.

Mouth: With sharp yarn needle and black yarn, beg at right corner of drawn mouth. Use a backstitch (page 45) to make mouth. Secure inside shoe and weave in ends.

Tongue: With sharp yarn needle and pink yarn, make a single lazy daisy stitch below center of mouth.

Adding the Soles

Make and attach leather soles, referring to "Soles" on page 37 for complete instructions.

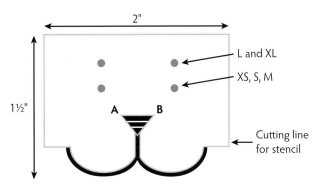

Felting

Felting is wonderful fun! With every project, I wait in front of my washing machine listening for the "finish" click, eager to take out my project and see the results. Once you've tried it, you, too, will be hooked.

The felting process used in these patterns, also called "wet felting," relies on movement and moisture to activate the natural scales and kinks in animal fibers, locking them together. The agitation and the friction created by the washing machine combine with hot water and detergent to transform the wool fibers into a beautiful, thick, compact fabric called felt.

Many factors can affect your felting results: the weight, twist, source of the wool, the dye used on the yarn, water temperature, front- versus top-loading washing machines, and even where in the washing machine your project ends up spending the most time. Through the felting process, the little shoes will shrink by approximately a third of their finished measurement after crocheting.

Size	Before Felting	After Felting
XS (0–3 months)	5½"	3¾"
S (3–6 months)	6"	4¼"
M (6–12 months)	6½"	4½"
L (12–18 months)	7½"	4¾"
XL (18–24 months)	8½"	5¼"

Materials for Felting

1 tube of foam pipe insulation in each of the two diameters listed for your size shoe (½" and ¾" or ¾" and 1"); see charts for "First Felting: Foam-Form Measurements" and "Second Felting: Foam-Form Measurements" on page 35.

Serrated knife

Scissors

Four large safety pins

Mesh laundry bag or zippered pillowcase

Washing machine; either top-loading or front loading will work

Laundry detergent

Preparing to Felt

Refer to the individual pattern for detailed instructions on sewing features before felting.

MAKING FOAM FORMS FOR FELTING

To ensure even felting in these little shoes and to help them keep their shape, I like to make a form from foam and stuff it into the shoes prior to washing. Tubular foam pipe insulation, available at most hardware and home-improvement stores, is perfect for creating inexpensive foam forms. Refer to the charts to determine the diameter of foam needed for the size shoes you're making.

The forms are held in place during the felting process by large safety pins at the opening of the little shoes. Because each pattern requires a minimum of two rounds of felting in the washing machine, you'll need two forms each in two sizes. After the first round, the shoes will have shrunk, so smaller forms are needed for the second round.

The length and diameter of foam needed are determined by the size of the little shoes. Use the charts below to find the width and length of foam needed for your project. Measure and cut two layers of foam insulation for each shoe for the first felting using a serrated knife. The inner foam will be longer than the outer layer by ¾", to make a rounded toe box in the shoe. Measure and cut the tubes for the second felting and set those aside.

First Felting: Foam-Form Measurements
For the first felting, you'll need two layers of foam to help shape the curved toe box of the shoes.

Shoe Size	Foam Piece 1 Length x Diameter	Foam Piece 2 Length x Diameter
XS	3¾" x ½"	3" x ¾"
S	4¼" x ½"	3½" x ¾"
M	4¾" x ½"	4" x ¾"
L	5¼" x ¾"	4½" x 1"
XL	5¾" x ¾"	5" x 1"

Second Felting: Foam-Form Measurements

Shoe Size	Length x Diameter of Foam
XS	3" x ½"
S	3½" x ½"
M	4" x ½"
L	4¾" x ¾"
XL	5¼" x ¾"

Use scissors to slice open the length of the foam tube for the inside layer (½"-diameter foam for sizes XS, S, and M, and ¾"-diameter foam for sizes L and XL). Roll the longer inner foam tightly and insert it with a twisting motion into the outer, shorter foam tube. This will be a tight fit. Using a drop or two of liquid dish soap diluted with water on the outside of the inner tube makes it easier to insert.

*1. First felting form   2. Second felting form
3. Cross section of first felting form*

Insert the smaller-diameter end of the form into the shoe all the way to the end of the toe box to prevent folds and creases. Keep the foam form in place by pinning the opening of the shoe as shown in the photo on page 36. Repeat for the second shoe.

MACHINE FELTING

Before felting, see "Last-Minute Checklist before Felting" on page 36. Put your form-stuffed shoes in a securely closed mesh bag or pillowcase and presoak in a bowl or bucket of the hottest tap water for several minutes to relax and saturate the fibers. Set your washer to the smallest load size with hot wash and cold rinse cycles, add a small amount of detergent, and put in the shoes, still in their bag or pillowcase. The bag promotes even felting and prevents the shoes from getting lost or stuck in the washing machine. Add an old pair of blue jeans to create some friction and encourage motion in the agitation. I have used both front- and top-loading washing machines for felting, and found that front loaders may require an additional wash.

After one cycle, remove the first felting forms and check the little shoes for size and shape. Examine the toe box for any rascally creases, and smooth these out with your fingers or a wooden spoon as much as possible. Stuff the second felting forms into the shoes and pin shoes closed as you did with the first felting forms. If there was a crease, pin that area open and into the form with a safety pin. Repeat the felting process until you reach the correct measurement. With a front-loader machine, it usually takes two times for sizes XS and S, three times for sizes M, L, and XL. Variables in the wool, mentioned earlier, as well as doing multiple pairs of shoes at once, can affect the outcome. Another run through the washer may be needed. It is better to *overfelt* your shoes than to *underfelt* them, as they will stretch.

DRYING

Now your little shoes are felted! Use the "length after felting" guide in the pattern (also shown on page 34 in the chart "Size Before Felting/After Felting") and shape your little shoes to the right length and width. You may need to stretch them out a little. A wooden spoon does the trick to form the toe box.

Lay the felted pieces on a dry towel or flat drying rack. Setting the shoes on an active heat vent is useful for speeding up drying time. Make sure your shoes are thoroughly dry before proceeding to the next step in the pattern! This may take 24 hours or longer.

Unwanted creases or ear twists can be dampened and reshaped, using your fingers or the foam forms, and set to re-dry. If you are lucky enough to own a handheld electric fabric steamer, you can put it to use here.

Refer to the pattern instructions to apply embroidery details on your little shoes.

Shoe on the left is ready for felting; shoe on the right has been through the felting process.

Soles

Good soles, solidly stitched and made of quality materials, are a defining feature of these shoes. Your baby or toddler will wear them comfortably for a long time, and maybe hand them down to a lucky sibling, if you use the right materials and follow the keys to sole success.

Materials

Leather, ideally 3.5- or 4-ounce split cowhide, for soles. This weight lends structure to the shoe, yet is soft and flexible. It wears well, and the suede surface gives a little traction. Information on sources for this leather and alternatives can be found in "What You Will Need" on page 5 and "Online Sources" on page 48. A neutral gray, tan, or brown will look fine with all shoe styles, but if you'd like colorful bottoms, you can dye the split leather using fabric dye. Soak the cut and punched leather sole pieces first, and then follow the manufacturer's instructions on the dye package.

Tracing or tissue paper to trace sole pattern. You can also use clear scrap plastic.

Light cardboard such as a recycled cereal box, for making the sole template.

Paper hole punch, 1⁄16" or 1⁄8", to punch holes in your cardboard template. Or use a nail and hammer or mallet to make holes.

Marker for tracing sole pattern onto tracing paper and for transferring the pattern onto leather. You can use a fine-point permanent marker or a disappearing-ink pen.

Heavy-duty scissors for cutting leather.

Leather hole punch, or awl, to punch holes in the leather soles. If you prefer, you can use a mallet or hammer and a nail or awl, along with a cutting board or piece of scrap wood. If you purchase a leather hole punch, the best type to use for this project is the Tandy Leather Hole Punch set. It's like a screwdriver, with several tube tips to make different-sized holes. You only need one hole size—3⁄32"—for the soles of the shoes.

Scrap wood or hard-plastic cutting board for pounding on when making holes in leather.

Ball-head straight pins for marking center points on sole.

Sharp yarn needle to sew leather sole to shoe.

Worsted-weight 100% wool yarn to stitch leather sole to base of shoe. You can use the same color as the shoe or a contrast color.

Preparing the Leather Soles

The length of the soles will be slightly larger than the felted shoes. The resulting shoe will be neater if you stretch the felted shoe slightly during the sewing process. Trace the pattern for your shoe size (pages 46 and 47) onto clear scrap plastic or onto tracing paper and cut it out. Staple the plastic or tracing paper pattern onto cardboard, and cut that out for your sole template. Right and left shoes are identical, so only one template is needed.

Trace two soles onto the leather. Poke the marker through the punched holes on the cardboard pattern to mark dots on the leather sole. Cut out the leather soles using heavy-duty scissors.

Be a Smooth (Scissors) Operator!

For a smooth, straight edge on your leather, keep your scissors in contact with the cutting line. Don't cut with more than the two-thirds of the blade closest to the handle. Open up the scissors, slide the scissors forward, and make the next cut.

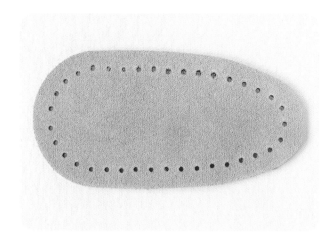

Using a leather hole punch, or an awl or nail and hammer, and a piece of wood or old hard-plastic cutting board as a hammering surface, punch out all of the little holes exactly where the dots are. Be sure to trim or brush away any tiny hanging bits of leather.

Attaching the Soles

Soles that are properly aligned and firmly affixed are important for the fit, comfort, stability, and wear of the little shoes. Take the time to attach them as neatly as you can, following the pointers given here. If you are even a little dissatisfied with how they look once you've sewn them on, take the stitching out and start over. Your trouble will be worth it.

Use straight pins to mark the center of the foot bottom and the centers of each of the side edges and toe and heel edges. This will help you align the sole perfectly.

Double-Check Before Stitching!

After pinning and before stitching, look at the shoes from all angles to see that the soles are well-centered and that they appear the same on both shoes.

Remove the pin from the center and pin the leather soles onto the shoes through the punched holes using your guide points.

Cut a length of yarn 10 times the length of the sole. Thread the yarn through your needle and tie a knot 8" from the end. This extra length will allow you to rethread it on the needle and weave it into the shoe at the very end.

Find the transition line between the crocheted sole and the upper portion of the crocheted shoe, about ⅛" beyond the leather sole. This is where you'll draw the needle through the shoe as you work the blanket stitch (page 45). At the center back of the heel, insert the needle from the inside of the shoe to the outside at the transition line. Then insert the needle into the leather hole, coming inside the shoe and out again at the point where the needle initially went through; this is the first stitch of the blanket stitch. For all subsequent stitches, insert the needle into the next hole on the right, coming out on the transition line outside of that hole and keeping the yarn behind your needle as it comes out. Continue, always holding the yarn behind your needle.

Continue with the blanket stitch all the way around your sole, being sure to draw the yarn *tight* with every stitch. After 6 or 7 stitches, assess your work. If the stitches don't look tight and even, use your needle to lift and tug the yarn between stitches, tightening them one by one, starting with your last assessment point. Is the sole snugly attached and well-centered? Use more pins if necessary to hold the sole in place more securely while sewing. Continue stitching, tugging each stitch tightly, all the way around the sole. The last stitch should go into the original hole you first drew your yarn out of, this time going from the outside into the shoe. On the inside of the shoe, draw your yarn tight and make a single knot.

and weave this yarn back and forth through the felting as well. Cut off the excess. One shoe is done. Finish the second shoe so it looks identical!

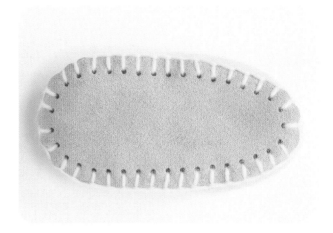

Weave the yarn tail through the felting back and forth a few times to make sure it doesn't come loose, and then cut the yarn close to the shoe. Thread the beginning tail onto the needle

Keys to Sole Success!

- Pin the soles in position on the shoes carefully, making sure each shoe looks like the other.
- When blanket stitching, draw the yarn tight! Tug the yarn with each stitch to make the blanket stitches as tight as possible.
- Recheck the position of the sole as you work to make sure it stays centered.
- Are your shoes virtually identical? They should be!

A Gift Insert to Copy and Give

If you're making the shoes as a gift, be sure to include this information on fitting and caring for the little shoes. You may photocopy this card or make your own.

 A GIFT FOR BABY
These cozy little shoes were made with love for

_____

To slip the shoes on your child easily, push the back of the heel down inside the shoe. Slide the child's foot all the way in so the toes touch the front of the shoe. With one finger, pop the heel back up into position. Machine wash cold, gentle cycle, inside a washing bag, no bleach. Reshape if needed and air-dry. The shoes can be resized by soaking the desired area with water. Wait a few minutes and gently stretch to the desired size. 100% wool, excluding soles.

Abbreviations and Basic Stitches

Here you'll find the abbreviations used in the patterns in this book, as well as instructions on how to do the basic crochet and embroidery stitches needed to make the little shoes. For those crafters who appreciate multimedia instruction, it can be informative and entertaining to look at tutorials on websites and video channels on the Internet.

Crochet Abbreviations

approx	approximately
beg	begin(ning)
ch(s)	chain(s) or chain stitch(es)
cont	continue(ing)(s)
dc	double crochet(s)
dc2tog	double crochet 2 stitches together— 1 stitch decreased
dec(s)	decrease(ing)(s)
g	gram(s)
inc(s)	increase(ing)(s)
m	meter(s)
mm	millimeter(s)
oz	ounce(s)
rem	remain(ing)
rep(s)	repeat(s)
RS	right side
sc	single crochet(s)
sc2tog	single crochet 2 stitches together— 1 stitch decreased
sk	skip
sl st(s)	slip stitch(es)
st(s)	stitch(es)
tog	together
tr	triple crochet(s)
WS	wrong side
yd(s)	yard(s)

Basic Crochet Stitches

Just a few simple stitches are all you need to make the shoes in this book.

Slip knot. Make a loop, and then hook another loop through it. Tighten gently and slide the knot up to the hook.

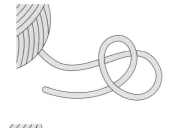

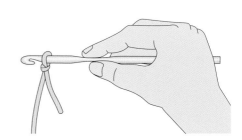

Chain stitch (ch). Yarn over the hook and draw the yarn through to form a new loop without tightening up the previous one. Repeat to form as many chain stitches as required. Do not count the slip knot as a stitch.

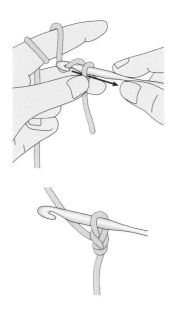

Slip stitch (sl st). This stitch is used for joining and shaping pieces. Insert the hook into the work (second chain from the hook), yarn over the hook, and draw the yarn through both the work and the loop on the hook in one movement.

Single crochet (sc). *Insert the hook into the work (second chain from the hook on a starting chain), yarn over the hook, and draw the yarn through the work only.

Yarn over the hook again and draw the yarn through both loops on the hook.* One single crochet made. For the next single crochet, repeat from * to *.

Double crochet (dc). *Yarn over the hook and insert the hook into the work (fourth chain from the hook on a starting chain).

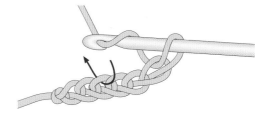

Yarn over the hook and draw through the work only. Yarn over the hook and draw through the first two loops only.

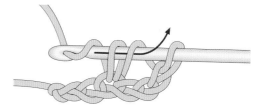

Yarn over the hook and draw through the last two loops on the hook.* One double crochet made. For the next double crochet, repeat from * to *.

Triple crochet (tr). *Yarn over the hook twice and insert the hook into the work (fourth chain from the hook on the starting chain). Yarn over the hook and draw through the work; four loops are on the hook. Yarn over the hook and draw through the first two loops; three loops are on the hook.

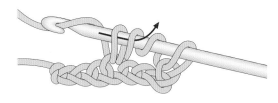

Yarn over the hook and draw through two loops; two loops are on the hook.

Yarn over the hook and draw through the last two loops on the hook.* Triple crochet is completed. For the next treble, repeat from * to*.

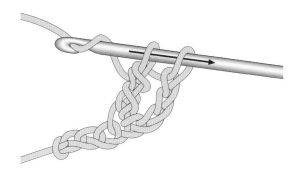

Single crochet decrease (sc2tog). *Insert the hook into the work. Yarn over the hook and draw the yarn through the work only. Two loops are on the hook. Insert the hook into the next stitch. Yarn over the hook and draw the yarn through the work. Three loops are on the hook. Yarn over the hook again and draw the yarn through all three loops.* One single crochet decrease is completed. For the next single crochet decrease, repeat from * to *.

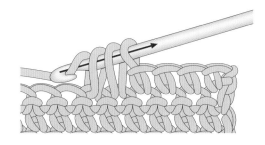

Double crochet decrease (dc2tog). *Yarn over the hook and insert the hook into the work. Yarn over the hook and draw through the work. Three loops are on the hook. Yarn over the hook and draw through the first two loops. Two loops are on the hook.

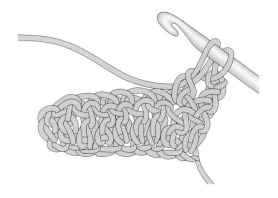

Yarn over the hook and insert the hook into the next stitch. Yarn over the hook and draw through the work. Four loops are on the hook.

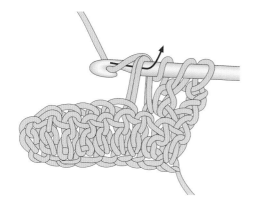

Yarn over the hook and draw through the first two loops on the hook. Three loops are on the hook.

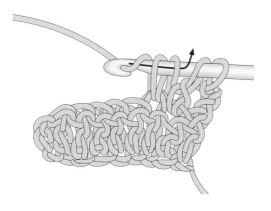

Yarn over the hook and draw through the last three loops on the hook.* One double crochet decrease is completed. For the next double crochet decrease, repeat from * to *.

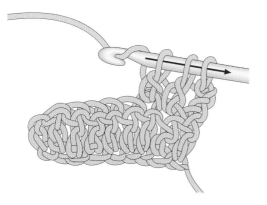

Double crochet decrease color change (dc2tog color change). This decrease is worked on a few projects when it's necessary to make a smooth outline between two colors. It is similar to the standard double crochet decrease just decribed, except that you'll drop the old color and pick up the new color before starting the second stitch of the decrease.

Using the old color, yarn over the hook and insert the hook into the work. Yarn over the hook and draw through the work. Three loops are on the hook. Yarn over the hook and draw through the first two loops. Two loops are on the hook. *Drop the old color. Pick up the new color,* yarn over the hook, and insert the hook into the next stitch. Yarn over the hook and draw through the work. Four loops are on the hook. Yarn over the hook and draw through the first two loops on the hook. Three loops are on the hook. Yarn over the hook and draw through the last three loops on the hook.

Special Techniques

If you're not familiar with basic crochet, you can download free, illustrated information at ShopMartingale.com/HowtoCrochet. There are a few special techniques you'll also need to know to make the shoes in this book.

ADJUSTABLE RING

The adjustable ring is an excellent way to begin the portions of the patterns, such as ears and eyes, that are crocheted in the round. It allows you to tighten the first row to close the center of the round nicely. Make a loop about 1" in diameter with your yarn, leaving a tail of at least 6".

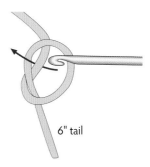

6" tail

Draw the working yarn through the loop with your crochet hook. Yarn over the hook and pull through the loop.

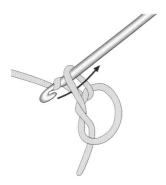

Work the required number of chains and crochet stitches as instructed in the pattern. Be sure to enclose both strands of yarn that form the ring. Pull the tail of the adjustable ring tight to close the hole.

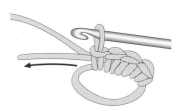

CHANGING COLOR

For a clean color transition, change the yarn on the last loops of a stitch. With the last two loops (three loops on a decreasing stitch) on the hook, tie the new color yarn to the existing yarn with a simple overhand knot, leaving a 6" tail for weaving. Bring the new color yarn over the hook and draw through the last loops. Color change is completed. At the end of crocheting, weave the tail ends into the fabric, like colors together.

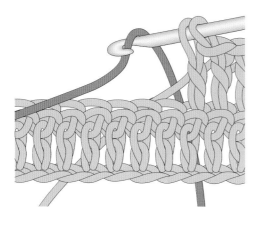

FASTENING OFF

When your work is completed, cut the yarn and draw it through the last loop. For the little shoes, leave a minimum of 6" for weaving. For ears, eyes, and patches, leave 12" for sewing.

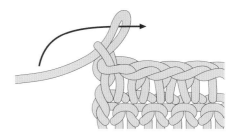

Basic Embroidery Stitches for Finishing

Always use a sharp needle to achieve well-defined stitching lines and precise placement. When threading a needle, leave a 6" tail of yarn before your knot. By threading this tail on your needle and weaving it in after you're done stitching, you will secure your work without the bulk of a big knot. At the end of your stitching, secure with a single knot on the inside, again leaving a 6" tail to thread onto the needle and weave it in. This will keep the inside of the little shoe smooth and comfortable on baby's foot.

Make a Face Stencil

A stencil is a great tool for making sure your two shoe faces match, and you can recycle clear-plastic packaging to make one. Cut a 2½" square of sturdy but flexible clear plastic. Some of the animal shoe styles in this book have traceable patterns so that you can make the faces on the animal shoes exactly as shown. Trace the pattern onto the plastic with a pen or pencil. If you'd prefer to design your own face, hold the plastic against the front of the shoe, and draw the desired facial features onto the plastic with a felt pen. Cut out the stencil with a utility knife or small nail scissors and mark the face on the little shoe using a regular or air-soluble pen.

BACKSTITCH

Use this stitch for mouths.

Pull the needle through from the wrong side to the front at A. Make a small backstitch entering at B and coming out again a little in front of first stitch at C. Make a second backstitch inserting needle again at A and coming out again a little in front of C, and continue.

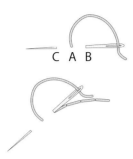

CHAIN STITCH

We used a chain stitch for antennae on the Ladybug shoe (page 17).

Pull the needle through from the inside to the front at A. Make a loop and insert the needle next to A, coming out again at B, holding the thread under the needle as you pull. Insert the needle again at B and continue.

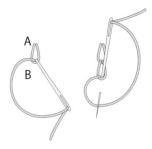

LAZY DAISY STITCH

Sometimes called the detached chain stitch, this stitch makes wonderful seeds, spots, and tongues.

Pull the needle through from the inside to the front at A. Make a loop and insert again right next to A. Come out again at B, holding the thread under the needle as you pull tight. The stitch will look like a petal. Insert the needle at C and move on to the next petal.

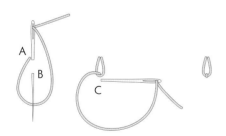

BLANKET STITCH

From the inside of the shoe, pull the needle through about ⅛" beyond the leather sole at A. Insert the needle at B (the leather hole) and come through at A again. Pull the stitch tight, insert the needle into the next hole to the right, and then come out at C, holding the yarn under your needle. Continue stitching, holding the yarn under the needle when it comes out. Use the blanket stitch along with additional detailed instructions in "Soles" on page 37.

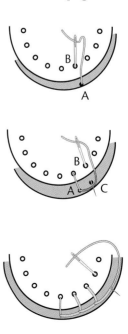

FRENCH KNOT

French knots are perfect for eyes.

Pull the needle through from the wrong side to the front. Holding the thread taut with your left hand, use your right hand (holding the needle) to wind the needle around the thread twice (A). Insert the needle back into the shoe (or fabric) at B, pulling the thread firmly to bring the knot flush against the fabric.

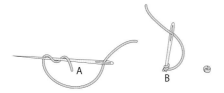

RUNNING STITCH

Also called the straight stitch, this is the most basic straight-line stitch and is used to attach smaller pieces to the shoes. Insert the needle over and under the fabric at evenly spaced intervals.

SATIN STITCH

This stitch is used for noses and mouths. Pull the needle through from the inside to the front at A. Take the needle back into the shoe at B and bring it back through to the front at C. Keep the stitches as parallel and as close together as possible. Avoid pulling the thread too tightly and keep a gentle, even tension.

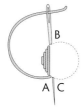

HEMSTITCH

This is the stitch used to attach ears, patches, spots, and Froggy eyes. Make sure that both shoes are right side out before beginning to sew. For information on placement of ears, eyes, and patches, refer to the specific pattern.

Use the long tail of yarn left from crocheting the pieces for sewing. For ears, begin with a few close stitches to secure the side of the ear. Begin with a single stitch for eyes and patches. Insert the needle into the shoe from the inside, pull through the edge of the ear, eye, or patch, go back into the shoe near but not into the same spot, and repeat, catching the ear, eye, or patch along the edge with each stitch. Continue to the end and secure the yarn with a small knot. Weave in the yarn end a few times to secure, and trim.

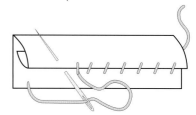

Sole Patterns

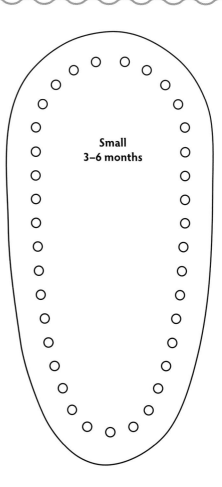

**Small
3–6 months**

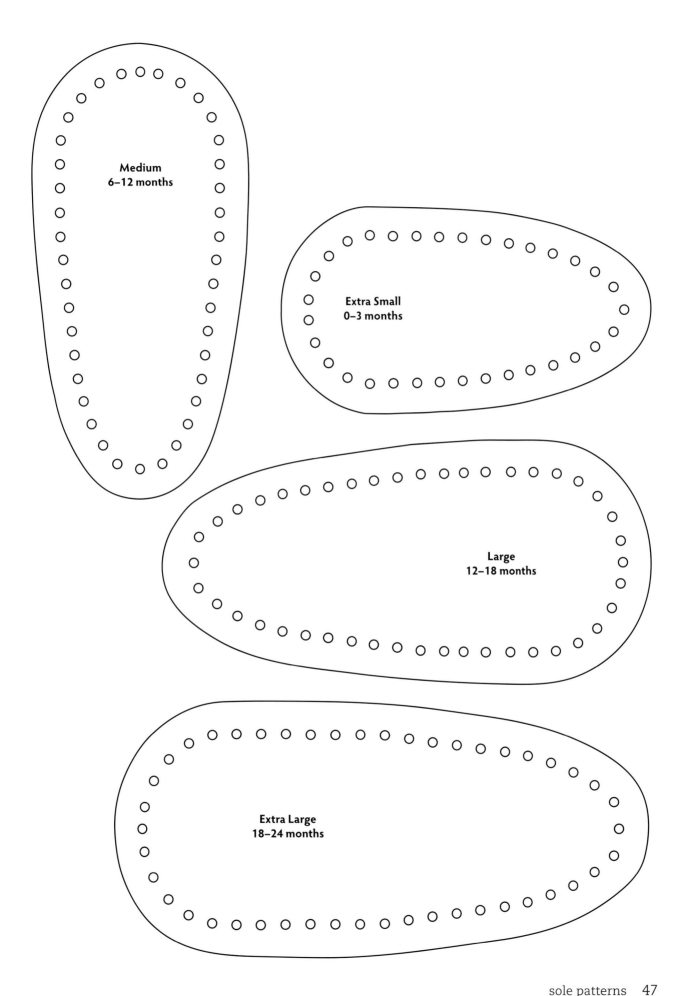

Medium
6–12 months

Extra Small
0–3 months

Large
12–18 months

Extra Large
18–24 months

About the Authors

Chantal Garceau is the founder of Chantal's Little Shoes, and the designer of all of these little shoes and more. After a career as a sportswear designer in Vancouver, British Columbia, Canada, she moved to Washington State and put her creative background to use as a freelancer for charity, and just for fun. In December of 2010, she began to sponsor a child with the Imani Project in Kenya, Africa. Learning about the great needs of orphan children in Kenya prompted her to start Chantal's Little Shoes, a social enterprise devoting all profits to this cause. Chantal lives in Woodinville, Washington, with her husband.

Mary J. King grew up in Minnesota and has dabbled in many arts and crafts, preferring to repurpose salvaged and secondhand materials whenever possible. She enjoys volunteering for a variety of causes, including Chantal's Little Shoes. Mary has degrees in languages and library science from the University of Minnesota, and writing has been a lifelong hobby and delight for her. She lives in Woodinville, Washington, with her family and pets.

Online Sources

Visit the websites of the following companies to order directly or to find shops that carry the materials featured in this book.

Cascade Yarns
www.cascadeyarns.com
Cascade 220 Wool

Frost King
www.frostking.com
Tubular foam pipe insulation

JoAnn
www.joann.com
Miscellaneous crochet and sewing supplies, including crochet hooks, comfort cushions, pins, needles, scissors, pens, chalk, markers, yarns, leather elbow patches, measuring tape

Patons
www.yarnspirations.com/patons
Classic Worsted Wool

Tandy Leather Factory
www.tandyleatherfactory.com
3.5- to 4-ounce split cowhide leather, other leather choices, and leather hole-punch set

Acknowledgments

We are grateful to Martingale for the opportunity to share these patterns and techniques to benefit the Imani Project, with special thanks to Karen Burns, Mary Green, Marcy Heffernan, Ursula Reikes, and Cathy Reitan. We are deeply indebted to the many volunteers who have kept Chantal's Little Shoes running by crocheting, labeling, packaging, cutting, stitching, smiling, and always encouraging us. Finally, our spouses, David Banton and Phil Nelson, cheerfully endured and forgave more than a few minor meltdowns during the writing of this book, and for that and more we are truly appreciative.